Vaping Home Brewers Recipe Collection
Compiled by Damien Smy

NOTES

84

General Information

Welcome to the Vaping Home Brewers Recipe Book.

This publication has been a community effort, put together by members of the Facebook group Vaping Home Brewers.

Experienced home brewers are free to ignore most of the small tips that are there to help those new to mixing, as well as the warnings, as, after all, everybody will have a different style, and process towards their mixing.

If you feel you may be able to add to the group, it can be found by searching Facebook for Vaping Home Brewers.

All Company Names are property, Copyright © or Trademark ™ of the relevant company, and are used without permission, affiliation, threat, or other derogatory use.

All these recipes are made through trial and error, and no guarantee is made that you will enjoy them as much as the creator.

Vaping is not recommended to those who have never smoked, and is intended to deliver nicotine in a safer manner than smoking.

All recipes that have been found in this publication can be found on the Vaping Home Brewers Facebook group, including either contributing member or source on where it was found. Unless otherwise stated, all recipes were created or found by Kal Morris, Admin of Vaping Home Brewers Group.

Cover Artwork courtesy of Paul Dolby

Foreword

My own mixing journey has been a somewhat slow and painful one I was mistaken in the early days, believing that you could just buy any ingredients and literally throw them together, as a result my mixes were somewhat dire and mostly unvapeable.

However I did become frustrated by my lack of results and decided the only real way to tackle the issue was by full research, several years later I am now producing quality juices for myself, close friends and vaping family members

The recipes contained in this publication are sourced from many places ,so credit needs to be given for those who put the groundwork in on developing the recipes and a big thanks for being willing to share with the vaping public

Credit also goes to the concentrate manufacturers for their development of concentrates suitable for the production of safe e-liquids. Lastly but not least credit goes to the people involved in making this publication available to us,and to the members of Vaping Home brewers for the interest they have shown in the group and their willingness to share their knowledge.

Kal

Steeping

What is steeping? Steeping is the process of allowing the flavours to mix, and combine to give the best possible taste.

How do you steep liquids? The best possible steeping method to leave a juice in a room temperature, dark place. This reduces the amount the nicotine from oxidising, and changing the colour of the juice. Some juices will darken over time, even without nicotine.

There are many methods people will attempt to use to speed steep their juices, such as using a slow cooker, a saucepan of water, a microwave, USB cup warmers, and possibly others we have not yet encountered.

There may be some truth to these, however, time is the best method out there.

If you do decide to try one of the heating methods, it is suggested that you leave the nicotine out of the juice until you have finished, as you will either break the nicotine down, or evaporate it, making it pointless having put it in, in the first place.

General Mixing Information

The mixing of e-cigarette juice should be undertaken on a non-porous surface, while wearing gloves suitable to protect your skin from contact with the liquids you are using.

Nicotine is a poison, it is toxic if swallowed or in contact with the skin. Please keep your concentrates locked up an away from children.

While mixing you may be using blunt needles with syringes. Please remember to treat these items with respect, they can still cause injury.

Please ensure that all your equipment has been sterilised in your preferred manner. For those that are new to mixing, you can sterilise your equipment in much the same way as you sterilise baby feeding equipment, such as steam, fluid, and boiling. Always select the most appropriate method for your equipment.

Nicotine and How to Store it

Nicotine WILL NOT degrade if it is 100% pure and nitrogen sealed in dark glass bottles and kept at a low temperature. That's how professional labs keep it so it's as close as a fact as you will get when it comes to nicotine storage! Obviously you aren't going to be able to achieve all those criteria at home (you wont have 100% pure nicotine being the main one) BUT majority of us could accomplish two of those important criteria.

Once you add other chemicals such as PG or VG into the bottle and can't remove all the oxygen then degradation occurs. At what rate and the effect is open to question as no one has actually kept PG or VG nicotine base in a freezer for more than about 5 years so far but it will degrade to some degree even if you do keep it in your freezer. The issue really is with the oxygen either from air trapped in the bottle or through energy put into the chemical system via light (UV) breaking down the dilutant (PG or VG), which unfortunately being organic compounds have oxygen in their make up. It's fine normally because the oxygen in the dilutant is attached to a hydrogen, making a diol (O-H) and will not compete for the nicotine but if you add energy into the system the one single covalent bond between the oxygen and the hydrogen can be broken and you have the issue of the spare oxygen running around causing problems. This is the reason to keep the nic base in amber glass bottles and is the same reason that nicotine is kept nitrogen sealed in labs - so there are no spare oxygen atoms. Keeping the nicotine base at low (freezer) temperatures also slows down the movement of the molecules, which obviously slows down any chemical reactions.

Oxygen is nicotine's main enemy, it converts it to nicotine oxide in an oxidation reaction and nicotine oxide being a charged molecule has free electrons, this is why the colour change occurs (free electron movement between the atomic energy levels). These free electrons can also target other substances in e-liquid such as flavourings and changes their chemical structure, which coincidentally is the reason why e-liquid has a shelf life.

Storage Basics

Always buy the highest percentage nicotine base you can buy (currently 7.2% (72mg) legally in the UK) as the less PG/VG you have in the bottle the better and always buy the best quality, freshest base you can find to start off with.

What to store it in?

Nicotine base should be stored in dark amber glass bottles to stop UV degradation and potential chemical leaching caused by plastic bottles.

How to store it?

Depending on your usage if you bought 1 litre+ bottles then you should decant it into smaller quantity bottles containing the amount you would probably use in 3 or 4 months so that you aren't exposing the majority of the nicotine base to more oxygen every time you want to use it. Once you open a bottle it's best to store it in a fridge if possible rather than just a shelf at room temperature and ALWAYS out of sunlight. It is worth noting that PG nicotine base remains fairly free flowing even straight out of the freezer but VG base turns into a gel and will need several hours at room temperature to be useable.

Where in the freezer to store it?

Purely from a safety point of view it is best to store it at the bottom of the freezer so that if it does leak it doesn't contaminate anything else in the freezer. I know that some people have a separate freezer for their nicotine base but plenty just stick it in with rest of the families shopping! Make sure that the bottle is clearly labelled, not for you but for the other people using the freezer. If you have young children it would be very wise, if not essential, to buy a small freezer to keep in the garage or similar just for your nicotine stocks.

What's better, PG or VG as the diluent?

A personal preference really but concerning degradation then VG has an extra O-H functional group (3 compared to 2 in PG) so it is possible that if degradation did take place it would be quicker in the VG. However VG has a better shelf life than PG, 2 years compared to 1 year generally AND VG's viscosity works in it's favour for once as the more viscous a liquid the less the molecules move about …… so it's probably 6 of one half a dozen of the other really as to which is best!

How long will it last?

It would be expected to possibly see and experience noticeable degradation after 5 -10 years storage either in taste or colour. Strength drop would need chemical analysis once someone has stored it for that long to determine but it is believed by many that it won't be anywhere near half.

What not to do

Leave the bottles alone! The less they are disturbed the better. DO NOT open the bottles if you don't need to and never shake them as this introduces oxygen to more of the nicotine base rather than just the surface.

I am not a qualified Industrial Chemist. This information has been obtained from conversations with qualified Industrial Chemists and personal experience and is for information only. I recommend you use this information as the basis for your own research rather than the definitive guide to Nicotine Base storage.

Common Abbreviations For Concentrate Manufacturers

CAP = Capella
INA =Inawera
TPA/TFA = The Perfumers Apprentice/ The Flavourers Apprentice
FA = Flavourart
FW = Flavourwest
DV = Decadant Vapours
M+P = Moms and Pops
OOO = One-on-One Flavours
PSV = Pink Spot Vapors
TP = Tasty Puff
CK = Classikool
TWG = Totally Wicked Gold
KH = Kandi-hed
LO = Lor Ann
FLV = Flavourah
CCW = Cup Cake World
CV/CC = Chef's Vapour Own/Chefs Choice
VV = Vampire Vapes

Guides To Average Mixing Percentages For Branded Concentrates

The following percentages are a guideline only sourced from user info and maker recommendations personal taste and mixing ratios play a great part.

CAPELLA
....

AMERETTO = 6%TO 8%
APPLE PIE =   7% TO 9%
BANANA   =   17% TO 21%
BLUEBERRY = 16% TO 20%
BANANA SPLT =7% TO 9%
BLUEBERRY = 16% TO 20%
BLUEBERRY CINNAMON CRUMBLE 8% TO 12%
BLUE RASPBERRY COTTON CANDY 8% TO 12%
BOSTON CREAM PIE =15% TO 20%
BULL HORN = 9% TO 12%
CAPPUCCINO = 10%TO 12%
CHERRY COLA =14% TO 16%
CHOC GLAZED DOUGHNUT = 8% TO 11%
CHOCOLATE FUDGE BROWNIE =8% TO 11%
CHOCOLATE RASPBERRY =18% TO 20%
CRANBERRY   = 10% TO 12%
DOUBLE CHOCOLATE MINT = 9% TO 11%
EGG NOG = 8% TO 10%
HOT COCOA = 7% TO 10%
IRISH CREAM = 6% TO 8%
POPCORN = 10 TO 12%
PINEAPPLE AND CREAM 8% TO 11%
SWEET GUAVA = 8% TO 10%
SWEET TANGERINE = 13% TO 16%
VANILLA CUPCAKE = 7% TO 10%
VANILLA CUSTARD = 12% TO 14%

DECADENT VAPOURS
....

ABSINTHE = 7% TO 8%
AMERICAN RED = 9% TO 12%
APPLE = 14% TO 16%
BANANA = 9% TO 11%
BLACK CHERRY = 9% TO 11%

BLACKCURRANT = 9% TO 11%
CARAMEL 10% TO 14%
CHERRY ICE = 11% TO 13%
CHOC CARAMEL = 12% TO 15%
COCCONUT ICE = 10% TO 12%
COLA KICK = 10% TO 12%
DY3 = 15%
DY4 = 15%
GINGERBREAD =11% TO 14%
LINE ZINGER = 11% TO 14%
PARMA VIOLET = 10% TO 12%
RASPBERRY = 12% TO 14%

FLAVOURART
....
ALMOND = 2% TO 5%
ANISE = 4% T0 6%
APPLE = 4% TO 6%
APRICOT = 3% TO 6%
BANANA = 4% TO 7%
BEER = 5%
BILBERRY = 2% TO 4%
BLACK CHERRY = 4% TO 6%
BLACK TEA = 4% TO 6%
BLACKBERRY = 3% TO 5%
BLACKCURRANT = 3% TO 5%
BRANDY = 2% TO 4%
BUTTERSCOTCH = 3% TO 5%
CAPPUCCINO = 4% TO 5%
CARAMEL = 4% TO 6%
CATALAN CREAM = 4% TO 6%
CHERRY = 6% TO 8%
CHOCOLATE = 5% TO 7%
CINNAMON =4% TO 5%
CITRUS MIX = 4% TO 8%
COCOA = 4% TO 6%
COCONUT = 6% TO 9%
COFFEE EXPRESSO = 2.5% TO 4.5%
COLA = 4% TO 7%
COOKIE = 3.5% TO 5.5%
CREAM FRESH = 4%
CREAM WHIPPED = 4%
CUSTARD = 5% TO 7%
FIG = 4% TO 5%

FOREST FRUIT 4% TO 7%
GREEN TEA = 3% TO 4%
GUAVA = 3% TO 5%
HAZELNUT =3% TO 5%
HONEY = 4% TO 6%
IRISH CREAM = 3% TO 4%
KIWI = 4% TO 5%
LICORICE = 4% TO 5%
COLD PRESSED LIME = 4%
LIME TAHITY = 3% TO 4%
LYCHEE = 4% TO 6%
MAD FRUIT = 5%
MANDARIN = 6%
MANGO = 5% TO 8%
MARSHMALLOW = 4% TO 5%
MENTHOL ARCTIC = 2% TO 4%
NUT MIX = 3%
ORANGE = 5% TO 6%
PASSION FRUIT = 4% TO 5%
PEACH = 4% TO 5%
PEANUT = 3% TO 5%
PEAR = 4% TO 7%
PEPPERMINT = 3% TO 5%
PINEAPPLE = 5% TO 9%
POMEGRANITE = 3% TO 4%
RASPBERRY = 6% TO 9%
RED BULL = 3% TO 5%
SPEARMINT = 5% TO 6%
STRAWBERRY = 2% TO 3.5%
TIRAMASU = 4% TO 6%
TUTTI FRUTTI = 2% TO 4%
VANILLA BOURBON = 5% TO 8%
WALNUT = 4% TO 6%
WHISKEY = 3% TO 4%

FlavourWEST
....
AMERICAN COKE = 12% TO 15%
APRICOT   = 14% TO 17%
BANANA = 12% TO 15%
BANANA FOSTER = 12% TO 15%
BANANA NUT BREAD = 9% TO 11 %
BLACK LICORICE = 11% TO 13%
BLACK CHERRY = 16% TO 18%

BUBBLE GUM = 14% TO 16%
BUTTER RUM = 10% TO 13%
BUTTER POPCORN = 10% TO 13%
CAKE YELLOW = 14% TO 16%
CAPPUCCINO = 11% TO 14%
CARAMEL CANDY = 14% TO 16%
CINNAMON RED HOT = 6% TO 8%
CINNAMON ROLL = 14% TO 16%
COCONUT CREAM PIE = 12% TO 15%
COFFEE = 9% TO 11%
COOKIES AND CREAM = 16% TO 20%
COTTON CANDY = 14% TO 16 %
CREAM SODA = 13% TO 15%
DOUBLE APPLE = 15% TO 17%
DOUBLEMINT GUM = 14% TO 16%
ECTO COOLER = 15% TO 18%
GUAVA = 11% TO 14%
GUMMY BEAR = 9% TO 11%
HAZELNUT = 12% TO 15%
JUNGLE JUICE = 12% TO 14%
KEY LIME = 15% TO 20%
LEMONADE = 9% TO 11%
0RANGE = 15% TO 17%
ORANGE DREAM BAR = 14% TO 16%
PEACH = 13% TO 16%
PEANUT BUTTER = 15% TO 18%
PINEAPPLE = 14% TO 16%
PINK CHAMPAGNE = 13% TO 15%
PLUMB = 13% TO 15%
RUBY RED GRAPEFRUIT = 13% TO 15%
SNICKERS TYPE = 14% TO 16%
SWISS CHERRY = 12% TO 15%
TANGERINE = 15% TO 18%
TROPICAL PUNCH = 14% TO 16%
VANILLA CUSTARD = 14% TO 16%
WAFFLE = 18% TO 20%
WHITE CHOCOLATE = 15% TO 18%

INAWERA FLAVOURS

BANANA = 4% TO 6%
BLACKBERRY = 4% TO 6%
CAPPUCCINO = 4% TO 6%
COLA = 3% TO 5%
COOL MINT = 3% TO 4%

HAZELNUT = 3% TO 5%
HONEY = 3% TO 4%
GRAPE = 3% TO 4%
LEMON = 3% TO 4%
MILK CHOCOLATE = 5% TO 8%
MINT = 3% TO 5%
NOUGAT = 6% TO 8%
ORANGE = 3.5% TO 4.5%
PEANUT = 3% TO 5%
PLUM = 4% TO 5%
RASPBERRY = 3% TO 5%
TWO APPLES = 4% TO 6%
LEMON = 4% TO 6%

THE PERFUMERS APPRENTICE

....

ABSINTHE = 5% TO 8%
APPLE = 12% TO 14%
BANANA CREAM = 15% TO 20%
BLACKBERRY = 14% TO 16%
BLACK CHERRY = 9% TO 12%
CARAMEL ORIGINAL = 16% TO 20%
CARAMEL CANDY = 15% to 18%
CHAI TEA = 8% TO 10%
CINNAMON DANISH = 8% TO 10%
COFFEE - 4% TO 7%
CREME DE MINT = 5% TO 7%
DRAGON FRUIT = 9% TO 11%
DOUBLE CHOCOLATE = 4% TO 6%
FRENCH VANILLA = 7% TO 10%
GINGERBREAD = 8% TO 11%
GRANNY SMITH = 7% TO 9%
GREEN TEA = 5% TO 7%
HAZELNUT = 9% TO 11%
HONEY = 6.5% TO 8.5%
LEMON = 9% TO 11%
MARY JANE = 14% TO 16%
MILK CHOCOLATE = 8% TO 11%
MOCHA = 5% TO 7%
PASSION FRUIT =9% TO 12%
PINEAPPLE = 11% TO 13%
PINA COLADA = 5% TO 6%
POPCORN = 14% TO 16%
RASPBERRY = 11% TO 14%

RIPE BANANA =14% TO 16%
RY4 = 13% TO 15%
STRAWBERRY AND CREAM = 9% TO 12%
WAFFEL = 10% TO 14%

TASTY PUFF

....

AWESOME APPLE = 2% TO 4%
BLUEBERRY THRILL = 3.5% TO 5%
CALIFORNIA ORANGE = 2% TO 3%
CHICK MAGNET CHERRY = 4% TO 4%
CHUMPY CHOCOLATE = 4% TO 5%
CHRONIC HYPNOTIC = 4% TO 5%
CONVICTED MELON (melone) = 4% TO 6%
CRAZY COCCONUT = 2% TO 4%
ELECTRIC BANANA = 4% TO 6%
FLOWER POWER = 3% TO 4%
JUNGLE JUICE = 4% TO 6%
MANGO TANGO = 4% TO 5%
MR BUBBLE = 4% TO 6%
PIMPY FRESH PEACH = 4% TO 6%
PURPLE HAZE = 3% TO 4%
RASTA ROOTBEER = 3% TO 4%
RIPPIN RASPBERRY = 4% TO 6%
SILLY STRAWBERRY = 3% TO 5%
SINFUL CINNAMON = 4% TO 5%
SPIFFY SPEARMINT = 3% TO 4%
TOKE A COLA = 5% TO 6%

TOTALLY WICKED GOLD

....

BLUE HAWAII = 5% TO 7%
ICE MENTHOL = 3% TO 4%
IRON BREWED = 3% TO 4%

Single Flavour Concentrates

(Credit Goes To Danial Carcas)

Single flavours and where they are from
%is how much % of flavour to base

✔ means mixed by myself and tastes good
X means tasted bad
The number at the end is steep time (DAYS)

All PG/VG Ratio for these are 40/60
If you want a higher VG ratio then you may have to up the percentage and vice versa
ALL MIXES ARE LEFT OPEN TO AIR FOR 24HRS

Vampire vapes:

Heisenberg	12%	✔	2
Pinkman	12%	✔	2
Vamp toes	12%	✔	2
Attraction	12%	✔	2
Bat juice	12%	✔	2

Vape domain:

Dragons blood	15%	✔	2
Strawberry lime kopparberg	12%	✔	3
Blue slush	12%	✔	2
Lilt	14%	✔	3
Wham bar	12%	✔	2
Millions	12%	✔	2
Mixed fruit kopparberg	12%	✔	2

Kandi Head:

Blueberry lemonade	12%	✔	2
Blackcurrant liq	10%	✔	X

Flavour west:

Green goblin	13%	✔	2
beetle juice	13%	✔	2
jungle juice	13%	✔	2
Cherry crush	12%	✔	3
Cream soda	12%	✔	X
Mt dew	12%	✔	2
Skittles	12%	✔	2
Unicorn vomit	12%	✔	7-10
Tiki roar	12%	✔	5
Watermelon candy	12%	✔	3
Apple jacks	10%	✔	9

One-on-one:

Pink lemonade	13%	✔	2
strawberry lemonade	14%	✔	2
Blueberry yog	13%	✔	14
Malted milk	12%	✔	X
Cocopops	12%	✔	14 X
Orange sherbet ice cream	12%	✔	4
Apple candy	12%	✔	2
Gummy fish candy	12%	✔	2

The Perfume Apprentice:

Berry crunch	12%	✔	14
Pear candy	12%	✔	2
Silly rabbit	12%	✔	9
Fruit circles	12%	✔	9
Hawaiian punch	14%	✔	2
Mount baker:			
Raspberry lemonade	12%	✔	2
Blue moo	12%	✔	14

| Fruity hoops | 10% | ✔ | 9 |

<u>Chefs vapor:</u>

Banana martini	10% ✔
Peach martini	10% ✔
Mango martini	10% ✔

Make Your Own Concentrates

Coffee

Take a 30ml plastic bottle and fill to the 1/3rd mark with your favourite coffee then top the bottle up to the shoulder with PG. Stand in a pan of lightly simmering water for 15 mins while shaking the bottle hard every 5 mins.

Filter the mix into a clean container using a coffee filter paper twice, then put it back in the simmering water for a further 15 mins. Finally filter it once more, rebottle the mix and steep in a dark place for 2 weeks.

You now have a coffee concentrate. How much you use in a mix is dependant on personal taste and the strength of the coffee uses but i use about 8%

Vanilla

To make Vanilla concentrate slice two pods don't cut them up just slice from one end to the other and leave in 20ml of PG and put in a dark draw for two weeks + by the way a test tube with a rubber stopper is best for this as the pods are long like sticks.

Menthol

Half fill a 10ml bottle with crushed menthol crystals, then fill it full of PG. Shake like crazy until crystals have dissolved (some people will use a hot water bath to help with the dissolving) then use just a couple of drops per ml of juice. Use PG, as the menthol is far less likely to recrystallise than if you use VG.

Recipes

Now to the part that you have all been waiting for.

On the following pages, you will find the recipes grouped by category.
This should make them easier to find, if you know where to look by type.

Please ensure, if using concentrates from different sources than those
listed, that you check the ingredients, and do not use anything that contains
any kind of oil. Pay particular attention to Lemon flavours, as they tend to
use the oil from the skin for the flavours.

Where you see EM, that is short for Ethyl Maltol which is a sweetener.

Drinks Or Alcohol Inspired Recipes

VANILLA CHAI LATTE
Black Tea (FA) 1-2% (from barely there to definite tea)
Vienna Cream (FA) 1%
Vanilla Tahity (FA) .5% (other FA vanillas will also work)
Cardamon (FA) .5%
Cinnamon (FA) .5%
Anise (FA) .5%
Clove (FA) .5%
** Honey (FA) .15% - measure carefully, but definitely include it! **
....

POMEGANITE CHERRYADE
Black Cherry (TFA) 2%
Cherry (LO) 6%
Pomegranate (LO) 7%
Sweetener (TFA) 3.5%
Tart and Sour (LO) 1.5%
....

APRICOT BRANDY
Apricot (TFA) 9%
Brandy (TFA/FW) 5%
Honey (TFA/FW) 2%
Lemon (TFA) 1%
Sweetener (TFA) 3%
....

SUMMERADE
Watermelon (TFA) 10%
Mango (TFA) 8%
Lemon (INA) 3%
Lemonade (FW) 5%
NOTE IF YOU WANT A COOLING SENSATION ADD SOME
KOOLADA AT BETWEEN 0.5 % AND 1.5%
....

Ok tiny mixing percentages but it is FA

IRISH CREAM MILKSHAKE
Irish Cream (FA) .5%
Fresh Cream (FA) .5%
Caramel (FA) .5%
Vienna Cream (FA) .5%

....

RASPBERRY LEMONADE

Lemon TPA at 7%
raspberry CLASSIKOOL at 8%
EM at 0.5%

....

ICY BLUE
Raspberry (CLASSIKOOL) 13%
Blueberry Wild (tfa) 4%
Citrus Punch (tfa) 1%
MENTHOL 1% TO 1.5% ACCORDING TO TASTE

....

CHERRY AMERETTO
9% LO Cherry
9% LO Amaretto
SWEETEN TO TASTE AND MIN 7 DAY STEEP

....

Tasty STRAWBERRY MILKSHAKE
CAP strawberries and cream 4 %
CAP sweet strawberry 3 %
TFA strawberry 3 %
TFA ripe strawberry 3 %
CAP vanilla custard v2 2 %

14 day steep is advised

....

RIGHTWAY

Absinthe (TFA) 2 %
Irish Cream (TFA/) 6 %
Green Apple (TFA) 6 %
Toasted Almond (TFA) 2 %
Whiskey (FW/INA) 2 %
Bitter Wizard (FA) 2 %

....

STRAWBERRY SODA

Cola (TFA) 7 %
Strawberry (LO) 11 %
Sweetener (TFA) 3.5 %
should be more or less shake and vape but i would give it 72 hours

....

STRAWBERRY LIMEADE
FA Lemon Sicily 1% of total
FA Lime Cold-Pressed 3% of total
TFA Strawberry (Ripe) 4% of total
48 HOUR STEEP

....

HARD LEMONADE
Lemonade (LA) 6 %
Kentucky Bourbon (TFA) 3 %
Vanillin 10% PG (TFA) 2 %
10 DAY STEEP IS ADVISED

....

XTREME COLA
Cola (TFA) 8 %
Cinnamon Spice (TFA) 4 %
Bavarian Cream (TFA) 4 %
Sweetener (TFA) 3.5 %
10 DAY STEEP AND AIR IS ADVISED

....

VIMTOISH
TPA gummy candy 7%
TPA grape 7%
EM....2 drops per 10ml
24 hour air and 7 day steep

....

KARAKOF CREAM (creamy caramel coffee)
Bavarian cream TPA 2.5%
Coffee with cream FW 7%
Caramel candy FW 5%
2 WEEKS MIN STEEP

....

BANANA MILKSHAKE (found this on a french site but i have tweaked
the percentages a little)
5% Ripe Banana TPA
4% Graham Cracker TPA
9% Malted Milk TPA
4% Vanilla bean ice cream TPA
2 drops per 10ml koolada

....

CHAMPERS
Champagne (TFA) 10%
Strawberry Ripe (TFA) 6%
Juicy Peach (TFA) 4%

....

Fruit/Fruity Style Recipes

Strawberry and banana

Strawberry (INA) 3%
Banana (INA) 3%

....

Bangin' orange

Orange (FW) 8%
Sweet Cream (TPA) 5%
Sweet Tangerine (CAP) 8%

....

SUMMER VAPE
Banana Cream (LA) 7%
Coconut (TPA)   4%
Dragonfruit (TPA)   4%
Pineapple (TPA)   2%
Strawberry (TPA)   4 %

....

PEARNANA (posted by kal)

This one is close to being a shake and vape.
Great after just 3 days in a cupboard or an hour in the hot pan.

Pear (TPA) 8.00%
Banana Cream (TPA) 8.00%

....

Lemon Lime Mint Recipe. Posted by Maxine Macaskill

6mg nic 10ml 80/20 vg:pg

Base: 0.83 ml
Pg/vg: 7.40 ml
Flavour: 1.80 ml

0.40 CAP Cool mint
1.40 CAP lemon lime
2 drops EM

Can shake and go but better after a slow cooker steep and cap off for 24 hours. Fine to sub ohm.
....

Triple Melon Mix. Maxine Macaskill

30ml 80/20 VG/PG 6mg

Base: 2.50mlVg/PG: 22.10ml

3ml CAP sweet melon
1.40ml CAP honeydew melon
1ml CAP cantaloupe melon
4 drops Ethyl Maltol
Steep time, one week.
....

WILD BUNCH
Blueberry Wild (TFA) 5%
Marshmallow (CAP) 2.5%
Sweetener (TFA) 2.5%
Wild Cherry (FW) 5%
Wild Strawberry (INA) 5%
....

PEAR TWIST
Pear (TFA) 10%
Bavarian Cream (TFA) 5%
Coconut Extra (TFA) 2%
Sweet Cream (TFA) 2%
Apricot(TFA)1%

....

APPLE ICE (simple)
16% TFA Apple
3% TFA Menthol
1% Ethyl Maltol

....

SIN CITY
Apple (TFA) 8%
Watermelon (TFA) 5%
Jolly Rancher (FW) 6%

....

ANGEL
TFA Flavours
2% Dulce de Leche
4% Ny Cheesecake
7% Sweet Strawberry
2% Raspberry
3% Peach
1.2% Ethyl Maltol
1% Smooth

....

Jade Tiger By Andrew Smith

To make 30.0mls @ 22.0mg Nicotine (Drops)
Base Nicotine - 9PG : - 9VG : 6
Coconut 12
Strawberry 42
Watermelon 36
Pineapple 30
Total Flavouring 6 Expected PG:VG Ratio - 50:50 Actual PG:VG Ratio -
50:50

....

The Kalsters Delight
Blue Raspberry Cotton Candy (CAP) 6%
Passionfruit (CAP) 5%
Grapefruit (CAP) 4%
Lemon Sicily (CAP) 5%

....

Tropical Cooler
6% Mango (TPA/TFA)
5% Passion Fruit (TPA/TFA)
3% Pineapple (TPA/TFA)
menthol to taste i use 0.8% of the very strong (INA) menthol

....

HEAVEN CAN WAIT
Ethyl Maltol 1.5%
Key Lime (FW) 3%
Lime Tahiti (FA) 2%
Nectarine (TPA) 4%
Strawberries and Cream (CAP)4%
Sweet Strawberry (CAP) 5%
ADVICE WITH THIS IS NOT TO GO ABOVE 70 VG

....

ORANGE WITH A TWIST
Bavarian Cream (TPA) 3%
Cotton Candy (TPA) 2%
MTS Vape Wizard (FA) 0.5%
Orange mandarin (TFA) 5%
Orange Mango (CAP) 4%
Sour (TPA) 0.5%
Stevia Sweetener 0.5%
Strawberry (Ripe) (TPA) 4%

....

BLUEBERRY BOOGER
Blueberry (CAP) or (CK) 8 %
Acai (FW) 4 %

....

CRYSTAL LITE
6.5% TFA Coconut
3% TFA Pineapple
2% TFA Coconut Candy
4% TFA Golden Pineapple
2.5% TFA Pear
2% TFA Whipped Cream

10 days steep is minimum

....

KALBERRY
Blueberry (LAN) 6%
Cranberry (TFA) 4%
Raspberry (LAN) 4%
Strawberry (LAN) 5%
Sweet Cream (TFA) 2%
Sweeten to taste
....

BSC - Banana,Strawberries and Cream
8% (CAP) Banana
6% (CAP) Strawberries & Cream
....

Melon Chill Posted By Lee Scaife
8% watermelon (PA)
8% honeydew (CAP)
2% peppermint (CAP)
2% koolada
2% Ethyl Maltol

After 48hrs this is really good, based on max vg.
....

Mimto
10% Vimto (20 sec vapes)
2% Menthol (Homemade, full tub of crystals in 30ml PG)
....

Joseph Francis
VANILLA BEAN ICE CREAM (CAP)10%
ORANGE CREAM (TPA) 4%
WHITE CHOC (TPA) 3%
CUSTARD V1 (CAP) 1%
WHIPPED CREAM (TPA) 2%

....

STRAWPEARY
TFA Honeydew 3%
TFA Strawberry (Ripe) 3%
TFA Pear 6%

12 hours airing followed by 24 hours steeping should be perfect

....

CREAMY MANGO AND PINEAPPLE
Bavarian Cream (TPA) 5%
Mango (FW) 5%
Pineapple (FA) 3%
Vanilla Cupcake (CAP) 1.5%

2 WEEKS STEEP IS ADVISED

....

GONE BANANAS
Banana (LAN) 6 %
Banana (FW/CAP) 5%
Ripe Banana (TFA) 4%
Sweetener (TFA) 3.5%

48 HOUR RECOMMENDED STEEPING AND AIRING

....

WILD BUNCH
Blueberry Wild (TFA) 5%
Marshmallow (CAP) 2.5%
Sweetener (TFA) 2.5%
Wild Cherry (FW) 5%
Wild Strawberry (INA) 5%

Minimum 7 day steep and air

....

RED ,BLUE AND PEACHY
TFA Peach (Juicy) 6% of total
TFA Blueberry Flavour (Extra) 6% of total
TFA Strawberry (Ripe) 6% of total

24 HOURS AIRING AND A WEEKS STEEPING

....

STRANGELY STRAWBERRY
(CAP) cucumber 0.3%
(FA) Strawberry 1.25%
(CAP)sweet strawberry 7.5%

12 hour airing followed by 24 steeping this should be ready to go

....

BERRY MEDLEY YOGHURT
TFA Blue Raspberry 3.50%
TFA Blueberry (Extra) 3.50%
TFA Strawberry (Ripe) 3.50%
TFA Bavarian Cream 2%
Capella Vanilla Custard v2 2%
TFA Sweetener 2%
Vanilla Swirl (TFA) 2%
Yogurt Flavour (TFA)5%
4-6 WEEKS STEEPING

....

PINEAPPLE CREAM
TFA Whipped Cream 3%
TFA Sweet Cream 5%
CAP golden pineapple 11%

24 hours air and a 10 day steep with this amount of cream to allow the fruit
to come through

....

COOL BANANA (24 hours air followed by 48 hour steep)
TFA Koolada 0.50%
FW banana 4%
CAP banana 8%
TFA Marshmallow 2%

....

BANGIN ORANGE
CAP orange 7%
CAP sweet tangerine 8%
KH orange tick tac 2 %
TPA sweet cream 3%

2 weeks to steep fully

....

VACATION MIX
CAP golden pineapple 2.5%
TFA Kiwi (Double) 2%
TFA Green Apple 1.5%
TFA Dragonfruit 3%
CAP guava 2%
TFA Pina Colada Flavour 7%

24 HOURS BREATHING AND 48 HOUR STEEP

....

CHERRY SUGAR
TFA Sweet Raspberry 1%
TFA Sour 1%
FW blueberry cotton candy 4%
DV sour cherry 5%

....

JUiCY FRUIT CHEWING GUM Posted By Joe Nukem (Warning: Very good ADV)
TFA Pineapple 10%
CAP Banana 10%

Leave to steep 2-3 days for best results (Smells and tastes just like the Gum)

....

BANGIN BANANA MILK
Ripe Banana (TPA/TFA) 5%
Graham Cracker (TPA/TFA) 4%
Malted Milk (TPA/TFA) 8%
Vanilla Bean Ice Cream (TPA/TFA) 6%

....

VOODOO
Sweetener - TFA 3.5%
TFA Juicy Peach Flavour 11%
TFA Raspberry (Sweet) 5%

24 HOURS AIR WITH CAPS AND NIPPLES OFF FOLLOWED BY 48
HOURS STEEP IN A DARK PLACE. YOU CAN ALSO ADD A LITTLE
KOOLADA IF YOU WISH

....

STRAWBERRY AND BANANA SMOOTHIE
TPA - Banana Cream 9%
TPA - Ripe Strawberry 8%
TPA - Sweet Cream 3%
TPA - Dairy Milk 1%

....

HULDRA
Acai, FW 4.5 %
BlueBerry, FW 4.5%
BlackBerry, FW 4.5%
Mango, FW 2%
Pomegranate, FW 4.5%

....

STRAWBERRY DRAGON
Bavarian Cream (TPA) 2%
Dragon Fruit (FW) 8%
Ethyl Maltol 10% (TPA) 1%
Koolada (TPA) 1%
Strawberry Sweet (CAP) 5%
Vanilla Swirl (TPA) 1%
Whipped Cream (TPA) 1%

....

KAL'S KANDY
2% TFA cantaloupe
1.25% FA Custard
1% FA Papaya
0.5% FA Mango
1% FA strawberry
0.5% FA kiwi
sweeten to taste

....

RED PUNCH
Grenadine (CAP) 3%
Dragonfruit (TFA) 3%
Blackberry (CAP) 2%
Black Currant (TFA) 3%
Hawaiian Punch (TFA) 3%
Sweetener (TFA) 3%

Yoghurt,Cereal and Milk Style Recipes

EXPLOSION
FW Strawberry 7.5%
FW Milk 4%
FW Vanilla cup cake 6%
FW Fruit Rings 4.5%

....

CRUNCHBERRIES RECIPE posted by Ash Ley
ALL TPA/TFA
10% strawberry ripe
5% cheesecake graham crust
6% Bavarian cream
2% French vanilla (I used deluxe)

STEEP FOR 1 WEEK

Originally found on reddit
....

STRAWBERRY YOGURT
CAP Creamy Yogurt 5%
CAP Sweet Strawberry 4%
TFA Strawberry (Ripe) 4%
FA Meringue 0.5%
FA Caramel 0.5%
TFA / CAP Ethyl Maltol 1%

....

HONEY NUT CHEERIOS
2% FW Hazelnut
1.5% FA Meringue
2% FW Yellow Cake
2% FA Marzipan
0.7% TFA Acetyl Pyrazine
0.4% FA Honey (might be a little much for some, maybe start with 0.2 and increase if you want to)
2% FW Milk
1% TFA Almond Amaretto
2% TFA Strawberry Ripe
1% TFA Sweetener

....

Shake & Vape Recipes

Bat Juice
Bat Juice(VV)   15%   70%VG 30%PG   Left with lid off overnight and
shake well in morning

Strawkiwi - William Cannon
Kiwi(TFA) 2.5%
Strawberry(TFA) 2%   Shake and vape is good but better after 1 night left
open to breath

Afro Red - Jennie Bell
TFA Red Astaire   10%   Breath 24 hours but can shake and vape!
TFA Afro Dizziac   3%

Coolberry - Jennie Bell
TFA Blackcurrant   10%
TFA Raspberry   6%
TFA Mentol   2%

Desert Style Recipes

CASTLEBROSIA ....AMBROSIA CLONE
12% Cinnamon Danish Swirl V2 Capella
2% Vannila CupCake TPA
2% Sweet Cream TPA
sweeten to taste min 14 day steep with this longer would be better

....

Strawberry Banana Cheesecake Posted by: Poyn2Ohmyvayp To your VG/
PG/Nic base add the following
5% Banana Cream (TFA)
5% Stawberry (Ripe) (TFA)
8% Cheesecake Graham Crust (TFA)
3% Whipped Cream (FW)
1% EM 10% (optional)

....

Sweet Honey Waffles by Andy Davis

Steep 4 separate batches of the following for 1-2 weeks - (patience is
needed for this one!):

Bavarian Cream (PA) @ 10% with 1ml EM
Molasses (PA)@ 10% with 1ml EM
Belgium Waffle (PA) @ 10% with 1ml EM
Honey (PA) @ 10% with 1ml EM

Personal preferred vg/pg ratio 50vg 50pg or higher vg

Wait a week or two...

Mix all these in 30% ratio each with just 10% honey (so for 30 ml use 9ml
of steeped Bavarian Cream, Molasses, Belgium waffle and 3 ml of Honey)
and let stand for another week or two..

....

Vanilla ice cream by Michael Lead
Kool effects 1% (FW)
French vanilla 8% (CAP)
Sweet cream 10% (CAP)
Marshmallow   11% (FW)
Coconut 6% (CAP)

....

Grants Vanilla Custard - (a different approach)

3% French Vanilla (CAP)
3% New York Cheesecake (CAP)
4% Vanilla Custard (CAP)
1% EM

....

Key Lime Pie

12% TFA Key Lime
2% TFA Caramel (Original)
2% TFA Vanilla (Bourbon)
1% TFA Sweetener
1% Lime Juice

....

Strawberry Cheesecake
NY Cheesecake (CAP) 14%
Sweet Strawberry (CAP) 7%
Marshmallow (CAP) 1%
Lemon Juice 1%
Ethyl Maltol 2%

....

RASPBERRY BASTARD (heavy steep required but delightful !)
Raspberry (CAP) 8%
Vanilla Custard (CAP) 6%
Chocolate Glazed Doughnut (CAP) 3%
Sweet Strawberry (CAP) 2%
Vape Wizard (FA) 1%

....

APRICOT PIE
Apricot (CAP) 2%
Almond (TFA) 1%
CDS (CAP) 1%
Whipped Cream (TFA) 1%
Vanillin (TFA) 1%
Graham Cracker (TFA) .5%
White Peach (FA) .5%
Cinnamon Ceylon (FA) .5%
EM 1%

....

GABBON (all TPA)
Apple Pie (TFA) 9%
Vanilla Bean Ice Cream (TFA) 5%
Caramel (TFA) 2.5%
Cotton Candy (TFA) 1.5%
Bavarian Cream (TFA) 1%
Graham Cracker (TFA) .8%

....

Park Avenue Vanilla Cheesecake
NY Cheesecake (CAP) 10%
French Vanilla (CAP) 5%

....

BUTTERSCOTCH DELIGHT (all flavourwest)
Butterscotch (FW) 8%
Caramel (FW) 3%
Fresh Cream (FW) 3%

....

RASPBERRY CUSTARD
Vanilla Custard (CAP) 11%
Raspberry (CAP) 6.5%
(a touch of EM say 0.3% is optional)

....

PEACH COFFEE CAKE
Juicy Peach (TFA) 10%
Cinnamon Coffee Cake (CAP) 2%
Toasted Marshmallow (TFA) 2%

....

Lemon Meringue Pie
4% FA Lemon Sicily
2% FA Custard
1% FA Meringue
0.5% FA Fresh Cream
0.5% FA Apple Pie
0.5% FA Cookie
0.5% FA Lime Cold-Pressed

....

BANOFEE
Banana FA 8%
English Toffee. LA 7%

....

CHOCCY CUSTARD
Vanilla Custard V1 (CAP) 11%
Toasted Marshmallow (TFA) 4%
Milk Chocolate (TFA) 5%
Chocolate (TFA) 5%

....

APPLE PIE DELUXE
Apple Pie (TFA) 12%
French Vanilla Deluxe (TFA) 3%
Whipped Cream (TFA) 2%
Caramel (TFA) 2%
Ethyl Maltol 1%

....

BAVARIAN CUSTARD
Bavarian Cream (TPA) 5%
Pralines and Cream (FW) 4%
Vanilla Custard v2 (CAP) 5%

....

MOMS PINEAPPLE CAKE
Cake Batter (CAP) 3%
Graham Cracker (TPA) 3%
New York Cheesecake (CAP) 2%
Pineapple (TPA) 2%
Vanilla Custard v1 (CAP) 4%

....

APPLES AND DIP CLONE (lickbrandvapors)
Butterscotch (FW) 8%
Fuji Apple (FA) 10%
EM 1%
This Is A 1.1 Clone

....

Vanilla Custard
9% vanilla custard (CAP)
2% smooth (TFA)
2% bavarian cream (TFA)
1.5% graham cracker (TFA)
1% catalan cream (FA)
1% butter (CAP)
1% eggnog (LA)

....

Toasted Marshmallow 6.75%
White Chocolate 5%
Vanilla Bean 3%
Sweetener 1%
Butterscotch 0.5%

....

TWINKIE
Yellow Cake (FW) 4 %
Vanilla Cupcake (TFA) 5 %
Bavarian Cream (TFA) 3 %
Sweet Cream (TFA) 3 %
Sweetener (TFA) 3 %

....

CREAMY CARAMEL
CAP Marshmallow 2%
FW dulce de leche 2%
FW salted caramel 5%
24 hours airing and 10 days steeping

....

PINEAPPLE CHEESECAKE
TFA French Vanilla 1%
CAP Golden Pineapple 5%
FA Vienna Cream 2%
CAP NY Cheesecake 4%

Sweeten to taste but this is nice after 3 weeks steeping
....

RED EYE
TFA Bavarian Cream 2%
CAP vanilla custard v1 7%
CAP sweet strawberry 1.5%
Ethyl Maltol 1 drop per 10ml

....

CHARLAS MILK
TFA Strawberry (Ripe) 9%
TFA Bavarian Cream 3%
TFA Vanilla Custard 3%
TFA Cheesecake (Graham Crust) 2%
TFA Sweet Cream 3%
....

BLACK FOREST CAKE
Jamaican Rum 1%
CAP V2 CUSTARD 2%
TFA Double Chocolate (Clear) 5%
TFA Whipped Cream Flavour 8%
TFA Maraschino Cherry 4.5%

2 WEEK STEEP ADVISED
....

Bendro's Strawberry Horchata:
TFA Sweet Cream - 5%
TFA Vanilla Bean Ice Cream - 4%
TFA DX Vanilla Cupcake - 3%
TFA Strawberry (not ripe) - 2%
TFA Marshmallow - 2%
TFA Horchata (not smooth) - 1%
FW Madagascar Vanilla - 1%

....

Tobacco Recipes

SMOKING SNAKE (TOBACCO RECPE)
TFA Honeydew 2.5%
TFA RY4 Double 2.5%
TFA Bavarian Cream 5%
TFA Pear 7% of total

5 DAY STEEP IT SHOULDN'T TASTE HARSH BUT IF IT DOES ADD
A COUPLE OF DROPS OF APPLE CIDER VINEGAR TO THE MIX IT
WILL SMOOTH IT
....

COFFEE AND A SMOKE !
Keoke Coffee (LA) 4%
RY4 (TPA) 4%
Toasted Almond (TPA) 2%
Tobacco Absolute 3.5%
....

Chris' Pub Vape:
3% Golden Rollie (FA)
0.5% Fuji Apple (FA)
2% Bavarian Cream (TPA)
2% Caramel (TPA)

*One for tobacco flavour lovers only
....

Gingerbread backy
FA golden Rollie 2%
Cap gingerbread 5%
MTS Vape wiz 1%

Steep 10 days minimum

Miscellaneous Recipes

THE TIDES OF MARCH
Pink Spot Rip Tide 10.00%
TFA Grape Candy 4.00%
KH Blue Raspberry 3.00%
CAP Blue Cotton Candy 2.00%
INA Menthol 1.00%

BETTER IF YOU DON'T GO TOO HIGH ON THE VG SO NOT A
CLOUD CHASERS JUICE

....

PURPLE BEAR all TFA
Grape Juice (TFA) 12%
Gummy Candy (TFA) 8%
Koolada (TFA) 1.5%

....

DRUMMER GIRL
Vanilla Tahity (FA) 1%
Jamaican Rum (FA) 1%
Jasmine (FA) 1%
Ylang Ylang (FA) .5%
Caramel (FA) .25%

....

A PAIR OF DRAGONS
Pear (TFA) 7%
Marshmallow (TFA) 4%
Sweet Cream (TFA) 3%
Dragonfruit (TFA) 4%
Bavarian Cream (TFA) 1%
French Vanilla (TFA) 1%

THIS ONE DOES NEED A DECENT STEEP GIVE IT 21 TO 28 DAYS

....

JABBA JUICE
Pear (FA) 6%
Ripe Strawberry (TFA) 5%
Ripe Banana(TFA) 3%
Sour (TFA) 1%
Sweet Cream (TFA) 1%
Marshmallow (TFA) 1%
Honeydew (TFA) 1%
Banana Cream (TFA) .5%
Juicy Peach (TFA) .5%

....

GRAND MARINER
Brandy (FA) 2%
Orange (FA) 1.5%
Bergamot (FA) 1.5%
Custard (FA) 1.5%
Fresh Cream (FA) .5%

....

FREYA
CAP-Sweet Strawberry- 9%
CK-Blueberry -8%
TFA-Sweet Cream - 3%
TFA-Dolce De Lychee- 2%
TFA-Vanilla Swirl -1%
Liquid Ethyl Maltol- 1%

....

SMARTIES (shell)
6% (TPA) strawberry
6% (TPA) tutti-frutti
4% (TPA) sweet tarts
4% (TPA) sour

This worked out very pleasant not authentic for smarties shell but fairly close and i mixed at 60pg 40 vg as i really wanted to sharpen those fruits
....

TOFFEE APPLE
8% Apple (LO)
6% Caramel Candy (FW)
6% Caramel (TPA/TFA)

....

SNOW BALLS
TFA Menthol 2%
Vanilla Custard (YOUR CHOICE) 3%
TFA Peppermint 6%

....

BLACK MENTHOL...Kal Morris
FA Blackcurrant 8%
FA Liquorice 2%
FA Menthol Artic 2%

....

GREEN GIRL
6.5% Fuji FA
1.75% Vanilla FA
3.25% Coconut FA

....

SKITTLES
Skits Candy (FW) 7.5 %
Rainbow Drops (TFA) 7.5 %
Cotton Candy (TFA) 1.5 %
Tart and Sour (LA) 0.5 %
Sweetener (TFA) 3 %

10 DAY STEEP IS ADVISED

....

VANANA NUT BREAD (REC STEEPING 48 HOURS)
TFA French Vanilla Flavour 5.5%
TFA Banana Nut Bread Flavour 16.5%

....

SWEDISH FISH

Swedish Fish (FW) 7.5 %
Swedish Gummy (TFA) 7.5 %
Cotton Candy (TFA) 1.5 %
Sweetener (TFA) 3.5 %
10 DAY STEEP IS RECOMMENDED

....

KALSTER VAPES - ICE ICE BABY
TFA Koolada 2% of total
TFA Menthol Liquid (PG) 2% of total
TFA Peppermint Flavour 10% of total

Great summer cooler or add an extra 1% menthol for a winter colds sinus clearer
please steep 48 hours

....

PEANUT BUTTER SURPRISE
TFA Toasted Marshmallow 2% of total
LA Peanut Butter 10% of total

10 DAY STEEP AND SHOULDN'T REALLY NEED SWEETENERS IF IT DOES PERHAPS A LITTLE ETHYL MALTOL

....

COOL MONSTER
monster energy 4% of total
TFA Sweet and Tart 2.50% of total
Ecto Cooler 5% of total
7 Day steep rec added in misc recipes

....

TRIX (Another i tried that worked out well)
TFA Lemon Lime 0.30%
TFA Cheesecake (Graham Crust) 0.60%
TFA Malted Milk Extra (Conc) 1.5 %
TFA Sweet Cream 5%
TFA Cotton Candy 3%
TFA Strawberry 5%
TFA Blueberry (Wild) 5%

....

GRINGO
Cinnamon Spice (TFA) 1%
Horchata Smooth (TFA) 6%
Malted Milk (TFA) 2%
Sweetener (TFA) 3%
Vanilla Swirl (TFA) 3%

....

MAN FLU CLONE
Honey and lemon menthol 15%
Menthol concentrate 1%
Absinthe 0.75%
Shake up and vape

....

CINNAMON TOAST CRUNCH
Cinnamon Danish Swirl V2 (CAP) 10%
Hazelnut (TFA) 1.5%
Malted Milk (TFA) 4%
Sweetener (TFA) 4%

Attributed to Tim Clinard at Facebook

....

LOVERS ROCK
Cinnamon Ceylon (FA) 10%
Vanilla Cupcake (TFA) 5%
Sweet Cream (FW) 5%

Attributed to vapechick at dot1ml.com

....

KALSTER VAPES
TPA Butterscotch - 7%
TPA Toasted Marshmallow - 2%
TPA Brown Sugar Extra - 1%
FA Caramel - 2%
CAP Vanilla Custard V1 - 4%
TPA Bavarian Cream - 2%

....

BLACKOUT
TFA Peanut Butter 8%
TFA Bavarian Cream 2%
TFA Graham Cracker 3%
TFA Brown Sugar Extra 1%
FW Hazelnut 1%
FA Caramel 1%
FA Torrone 0.25%

....

SINFUL CHERRY CREAM
6% Sweet Cream TFA
5% Black Cherry TFA
4% Bavarian Cream TFA
2% Vanilla Bean Ice Cream TFA
1% Maraschino Cherry TFA
1% Smooth TFA

....

LOFN (Goddess Of Forbidden Love)
Absinthe (TFA) 10%
Koolada 1%
Peppermint (TFA) 4%
Ethyl Maltol 2 drops per 10ml only

....

TRUE BLOOD
Strawberry (TFA) 6%
White Chocolate (TFA) 9%
Sweet Cream (TFA) 2%
Ethyl Maltol (TFA) 3%

Clone Recipes

All these recipes are clone of well known Premium e-Juice brands. These are created from tastes, and as such, you may notice a difference between the original and the clone.

Gambit clone

All TFA flavourings.

13.5% apple pie
5% pie crust
4% French vanilla deluxe
3% whipped cream
2% caramel

....

Suicide Bunny Original Bunny

10% Vanilla Custard TFA
7% Cake Batter CAP
4% Sweet Cream TFA
4% Bavarian Cream TFA

....

Mother's Milk Clone
3% CAP Cake Batter
15% CAP Sweet Strawberry
3.5% FW Bavarian Cream
1.5% TFA Ethyl Maltol
1% FA Smooth
1% FA Magic Mask

 *mix this using a coffee frother for a full ten minutes let it stand for an hour and then repeat the frothing and standing...steep in your normal method
....

BETTY CLONE (ALL FW APART FROM THE SMOOTH.EM ADDED TO PERSONAL TASTE)
Strawberry 5%
Pear 2%
Kiwi 3%
Pineapple 2%
Cantaloupe 2%
Guava 2%
Grapefruit 1%
Watermelon 2%
Peach 1%
Smooth 2% (TFA)

....
....

SNICKER DOODLE COOKIE CLONE

TFA Cinnamon Danish 8%
TFA Cinnamon Sugar Cookie 6%
FA Vanilla Tahity 2%
TFA Sweet Cream 2%
TFA Toasted Almond 1%

PG/VG ratio is either 70/30 or 60/40

....

PAPA SMURF CLONE
Pomegranate Deluxe (TFA) 7%
Blueberry (CK) 8%
Sweet Cream (TFA) 3%
Ethyl Maltol 2%

....

ROSTA BLOOD CLONE (AKA Bob Marley Blood)
Strawberries and Cream (TFA) 5%
Strawberry (TFA) 4%
White Chocolate (TFA) 8%
Mary Jane (TFA) 4%

....

COSMIC FOG MILK AND HONEY
Graham Cracker Clear (TFA) 5%
Marshmallow (TFA) 2%
Vanilla Swirl (TFA) 2%
Vanilla Custard (CAP) 2%
Peanut Butter (TFA) 1.4%

....

8 BALL CLONE
Banana Ripe (TFA) 4%
Caramel Original (TFA) 3%
Expresso (FA) 2%
Sweet Cream (TFA) 3%

....

QUEENSIDE (5 Pawns Clone)
French Vanilla (TFA) 10%
Orange Cream (TFA) 10%
Koolada (TFA) 1%

....

BLUE VOODOO FROM MISTER ELIQUID ..CLONE ALL TFA
Juicy Peach (TFA) 10%
Sweet Raspberry (TFA) 5%
Sweetener (TFA) 5%

....

PLUID clone
Absinthe (TFA) 1%
Horehound (TFA) 2%
Kiwi Double (TFA) 3%
Koolada (TFA) 1%
Marshmallow (LA) 2%
Orange Cream (TFA) 2%
Tangerine (TFA) 2%

....

BLUE VOODOO FROM MISTER ELIQUID ..CLONE ALL TFA
Juicy Peach (TFA) 10%
Sweet Raspberry (TFA) 5%
Sweetener (TFA) 5%

....

FIVE STARS FRUIT 0's (clone)
3% of TFA Sour
2% of TFA Acetyl Pyrazine
4.5% of TFA Bavarian Cream
9% of TFA Fruit Circles

....

SNICKER DOODLE COOKIE CLONE
TFA Cinnamon Danish 8%
TFA Cinnamon Sugar Cookie 6%
FA Vanilla Tahity 2%
TFA Sweet Cream 2%
TFA Toasted Almond 1%

PG/VG ratio is either 70/30 or 60/40

....

TNT CLONE
9% Strawberry Ripe (TFA)
4% Juicy Peach (CAP)
7% Double Apple (CAP)

....

UNICORN MILK
Bavarian Cream (TPA) 4%
Cheesecake (Graham Crust) (TPA) 5%
Marshmallow (TPA) 3.5%
Sweet Cream (TPA) 2%
Sweet Strawberry (CAP) 4.5%
Vanilla Custard v2 (CAP) 2%

....

BEARD VAPE No 5 Clone
New York Cheesecake (CAP) 10%
Sweet Strawberry (CAP) 5%

....

BEARD VAPE NO 32 CLONE
Banana Nut Bread (TPA)1%
Bavarian Cream (FW) 4%
Brown Sugar Extra (TPA) 1%
Cinnamon Churro (FW) 7.5%
Cinnamon Roll (FW) 7.5%

....

LOOPER CLONE
Bavarian Cream (TPA) 1%
Berry Crunch (TPA) 4%
Dairy Milk (TPA) 2%
Fruit Circles (TPA) 3%
Strawberry (Ripe) (TPA) 5%

....

HEISINBERG clone
Koolada 1%
Anise (Star) (TPA) 2%
Apple Double (TPA) 1%
Blue Raspberry (TPA) 4%
Blueberry Candy 8%
Bubblegum (TPA) 4%

....

DRAGONS BLOOD
TFA Bavarian Cream Flavour 2%
 Ethyl Maltol 1%
TFA Vanilla Swirl Flavour 3%
TFA Sweet Cream Flavour 1%
TFA Strawberry Flavour 4%
TFA Dragonfruit Flavour 10%

Alternative Recipe Tweaked For Dragons Blood

TFA Bavarian Cream 2%
Ethyl Matol   1%
TFA Vanilla Swirl   2%
TFA Strawberry   6%
TFA Dragon Fruit   10%

....

Betelgeuse - Nicoticket clone
Sweet Strawberry (CAP) 6%
Golden Pineapple (CAP) 5%
Raspberry (CAP) 5%
Sweet Mango (CAP) 3%
Sweetener (Sucralose) TFA @ 0.50% which is around 3-4 drops per 15ml.
(PG/VG Ratio = 65/35 to match the original

....

These four are based on a 10ml mix

SNAKEBITE CLONE

CAP Lemon Sicily total	Flavour 0.05ml	~1 drops	0.50% of
TFA Coconut Extra Flavour total	Flavour 0.10ml	~2 drops	1% of
TFA Bavarian Cream Flavour total	Flavour 0.30ml	~6 drops	3% of
TFA Green Apple Flavour total	Flavour 0.50ml	~10 drops	5% of

This recipe does not need to steep

UNICORN MILK

Dairy TFA total	Flavour 0.63ml	~13 drops	6.31% of
Sweet Cream TFA of total	Flavour 1.10ml	~22 drops	10.96%
CAP Sweet Strawberry	Flavour 1.99ml	~40 drops	19.93% of total

This recipe does not need to steep

COMET TRAILS CLONE

TFA Bavarian Cream Flavour	0.20ml ~4 drops	2% of total
CAP Vanilla Custard Flavour	0.20ml ~4 drops	2% of total
TFA Sweet Cream Flavour	0.20ml ~4 drops	2% of total
TFA Cotton Candy Flavour	0.15ml ~3 drops	1.50% of total
TFA Coconut Extra Flavour	0.15ml ~3 drops	1.50% of total
CAP Sweet Guava Flavour	0.80ml ~16 drops	8% of total

This recipe does not need to steep

....

Castle Long - Five Pawns clone
2.5% Kentucky Bourbon
1.5% Coconut Extra
1.5% Acetyl Pyrazine
1.5% Toasted Almond
1% Vanillin
1% Bourbon Vanilla
1% Brown Sugar Extra
All TFA Flavourings

....

Catherine The Grape From Velvet Cloud Clone

Start with PG/VG/Nic base of your choice.

FA - Black Currant..3 %
FA - Concord Grape 2%
EM added at 1 %

....

MILKMAN CLONE

All TFA

EM 3%
Strawberry Ripe 7%
DDL 2%
Malted Milk 3%
Cheesecake with Graham Crust 5%
Whipped Cream 2%
Vanilla Bean Ice-cream 5%
Sweetener 2 %

....

Derailed - Suicide Bunny (clone)
15% Sugar Cookie (FA)
5% Banana (CAP)
2% Cinnamon Danish (CAP)

....

MILKMAN CLONE
TFA Marshmallow 2.04% of total
TFA Vanilla Cupcake 1.63% of total
TFA Vanilla Custard 0.82% of total
TFA Sweetener 4.08% of total
TFA Whipped Cream 1.63% of total
CAP Sweet Strawberry 3.27% of total
TFA Ripe strawberry 4.90% of total

72 HOUR STEEP

....

Atomic Cinnacide (Tasty Vapor) Clone - Found By Chris Jungle..
0.5% Banana CAP
2% Bavarian Cream TPA
10% Cinnamon Red Hot TPA
1% Pie Crust TPA
4% Vanilla Swirl TPA

....

MUFFIN MAN CLONE
FA Fuji Apple 2.75%
FW Cinnamon Roll 5.50%

24 hours air and 7 day steeping

....

Cosmic Fog - Milk & Honey Clone Found By Chris Jungle:
8% Graham Cracker Clear
3% Marshmallow
2% Vanilla Swirl
2% Vanilla Custard
1.5% Peanut Butter
All TPA

....

Perpetual Check (Five Pawns) Clone, Found By Chris Jungle:
5% Cinnamon Ceylon - FA
2% Black Currant - FA
0.9% Fresh Fig - FA
1.25% Lemon Sicily - FA
0.75% Catalan Cream - FA
0.75% Vanilla Classic - FA
1.50% Brandy - SI (Signature)
0.50% Sucralose
0.25% Ethyl maltol

....

ANDROMEDA STYLE
TFA Blueberry (Wild) 6%
TFA Pomegranate 7%
TFA Sweet Cream 3%

2 week steep advised

....

CEREAL KILLA 9 South Vapes Clone
Bergamot (FA) 1.5%
Cake (Yellow) (FW) 2%
Hazelnut (FW) 2%
Lemon (FE) 3%
Lemon Meringue Pie (CAP) 0.5%
Meringue (FA) 2%
Orange (FA) 1%
Sucralose 1%
Sweet Tangerine (CAP) 1%

....

Dr.Jekyll - Digby's (CLONE)
Absinthe (DV) 6%
French Vanilla (TPA) 0.3%
Peppermint (TPA) 0.8%
Sweetener (Sucralose) (TPA) 2 .3%

....

Ambrosia - Elysian E-Lixirs (Clone)
12% Cinnamon Danish Swirl V2 (CAP)
2% Vanilla Cupcake (TFA)

....

Apple Cinnana - Fuzion Vapor (Clone)
Banana Cream (TFA) 8%
Strawberry Ripe (TFA) 8%
Apple (TFA) 6%
Ripe Banana (TFA) 0.5%
Cinnamon Red Hot (TFA) 0.5%
....

HALO TRIBECA (Clone)
10% Ethyl Maltol 3%
5% Acetyl Pyrazine 2%
TFA Graham Cracker 3%
TFA RY4 Double 13%
....

KARMA CREAM - Mr. Good Vape (CLONE)
Bavarian Cream (TFA) @ 3%
Cheesecake (Graham Crust) (TFA) @ 6%
Graham Cracker (TFA) @ 2%
Marshmallow (TFA) @ 2%
Strawberry Ripe (TFA) @ 6%
Peach & Cream (CA) @ 6%
Sweet Cream (TFA) @ 3%
Graham Cracker (TFA) @ 2%
Acentyl Pyrazine (TFA) @ 1%
EM @ 1%
....

MAN FLU CLONE Submitted By Don Wave Murphy
Honey And Lemon Menthol 15%
Menthol Concentrate 1%
Absinthe 0.75%

Shake up and vape - Chefs Vapour Brand Flavours
....

Kentucky Applewood - Vermillion River (Clone)
5% TPA Marshmellow
4% TPA Hazelnut
3% TPA Original Caramel
2% TPA Tobacco Blend
2% LA Apple
....

Madrina v2 - Suicide Bunny (clone)
(TFA) Cantaloupe 8%
(TFA) Jackfruit 1%
(TFA) Watermelon Candy 4%
Bavarian Cream 2%
Honeydew (TPA) 6%
Sweet Cream (TPA) 2%
60VG 40PG

....

Charlie's Chalk Dust Dream Cream Clone Found By Chris Jungle:

1% Sweet Tangerine - CA
1% Hazelnut - FW
2% Graham Cracker Clear - PA
12% Vanilla Custard - CA
1% Fresh Cream - FA
2% Bavarian Cream - PA

....

Bombies A Real Nightmare clone found by Chris Jungle:

4.50% Dutch Chocolate Mint - CAP
2.50% Mint Chocolate Chip - LOR
2% Cookie - FA
3% Graham Cracker - TPA
2.50% Mild Black - TPA
1.50% Root Beer - CAP
2% Double Chocolate (Dark) - TPA
0.50% Coffee - TPA
0.50% Espresso - TPA
0.66% Smooth - TPA

....

Space Jam Pluto (max VG for dripping) or for a tank @ 50/50
9% Honeydew (TPA)
4.5% Bubblegum (TPA)
0.5% Peppermint (TPA)
8% Honeydew (TPA)
4% Bubblegum (TPA)
0.5% Peppermint (TPA)

....

Mom's Pineapple Cake – EpiClouds (clone)
Cake Batter (CAP) 3%
Graham Cracker (TPA) 3%
New York Cheesecake (CAP) 2%
Pineapple (TPA) 2%
Vanilla Custard v1 (CAP) 4%
65VG 35PG

....

Omega Vape - Chronos clone found by Chris Jungle:
3% Butterscotch - FA
2% Bittersweet chocolate - FA
3% Madagascar Vanilla classic - FA
5% Marshmallow - FA
2% Meringue - FA

....

Cosmic Fog - Nutz clone found by Chris Jungle:
CAP Sweet Strawberry - 3%
TFA Ripe Strawberry - 4%
FA Meringue - 1%
FA Vienna Cream - 2%
FA Almond - 2%
FA Caramel - 1.5%
CAP Vanilla Custard - 1%
INA Biscuit - 2%
MTS Vape Wizard - 2 drops per 30ml

....

Summer Sweet - Velvet Cloud Vapor (clone)
Sweet Tea (CAP) @ 6%
Raspberry (TFA) @ 4%
Lemon (TFA) @ 3%
Sweetener (TFA) @ 2%
Sour (TFA) @ 1%

....

Lenola Cream – Kite in Cloud (clone)
LA Cheesecake - 3.5%
10% Vanilla in PG - 2.75%
INW Strawberry - 1%
FA Coconut- 2%
CAP Vanilla Custard V2 - 3%
70vg / 30pg

....

73

MOON SUGAR - Mr Good Vape (clone)
8% Graham cracker
4% Sugar Cookie
3% Caramel
1%-2% Ethyl Maltol

All concentrates are CAP

....

The Bell from H4KJUICE (clone) all TFA
Citrus Punch (TFA) 8%
Blueberry Wild (TFA) 8%
Key Lime (TFA) 2%
Menthol (TFA) 1.25%

....

Smurf Balls by Zeus Juice Clone TFA+LO
Sweet Cream (TFA) 10%
Blueberry (LO) 6%
Strawberry (LO) 4%

....

THE DUDE... alpha vape clone
Juicy Peach (TFA) @ 8%
Pineapple (TFA) @ 5%
EM (TFA) @ 3%
Mango (TFA) @ 2%

....

BEARD no 64 (clone)
10% Blue Raspberry Cotton Candy(CAP)
5% Hibiscus (CAP)

....

COSMIC FOG ...shocker (clone)
Lemon juice 1drop per 5ml
Ethyl Maltol 1%
Sour 0.3%
Strawberry Lemonade (FW) 10%
FIVE PAWNS 5th rank (clone)
3% Caramel Original (TPA)
3% Champagne (TPA)
4% Horehound (TPA)
1% Key Lime (TPA)
0.5% Menthol
1% Smooth (TPA)
4% Sweet Cream (TPA)
1% Sweetener (TPA)
1% Toasted Almond (TPA)
6% Vanilla bean ice cream

....

Alice In Vapeland ..White Rabbit (Clone) All TPA flavours
6% French vanilla
6% Marshmallow
4% whipped cream
2% sweet Cream
2% Coconut

....

CUTTWOOD BOSS RESERVE (clone)
Graham Cracker Clear (TFA) 3.3%
Caramel Original (TFA) 3.3%
Captain Crunch (FW) 3%
Peanut Butter (TFA) 3.3%
Vanilla Swirl (TFA) 2%
Vanilla Custard (TFA) 4%
Banana Cream (TFA) 10%
Cotton Candy/EM (TFA) 1%

....

CUTTWOOD ..SUGAR BEAR (CLONE)
4.8% Cinnamon Danish Swirl cap
8% Cinnamon Roll cap
3.2% Sugar Cookie tfa
1% em

....

75

SPACE JAM ...ECLIPSE (clone)
TFA Western - 10%
CAP Vanilla Custard V1 - 8%
CAP Marshmallow - 5%

....

FIVE PAWNS perpetual check (clone)
5% FA cinnamon ceylon
2% FA black currant
0.9% FA fresh fig
1.25% FA lemon sicily
0.75% FA catalan cream
0.75% FA vanilla classic
1.5% Signature brandy
0.5% sucralose
0.25% ethyl maltol

....

TIME BOMB TNT (clone)
9% Strawberry Ripe (TFA)
4% Juicy Peach (Cap)
7% Double Apple (Cap)

....

VAPOUR TRAILS SASQUATCH (CLONE)
TFA) blueberry wild - 8%
(TFA) Hazelnut - 2%
(Cap) sweet cream - 1.5%
(TFA) Bavarian cream - 2%

....

Mixing Suppliers

In the following sections you will find the most common suppliers that members of the Vaping Home Brewers group use for their supplies.

Alongside those recommended, you can also purchase miscellaneous supplies like syringes, blunt needles, measuring cylinders, mixing beakers and all sorts of other accessories to assist you from general retailers like Amazon, eBay, or any Pharmacy that stocks VG.

VG - Vegetable Glycerin

PG - Mono-Propylene Glycol

Nic - Nicotine Base, either VG or PG

PG, VG, Nic, and Concentrates:

http://www.valiant2vape.co.uk/

http://www.darkstarvapour.co.uk/

https://www.chefsvapour.co.uk/25-concentrates

http://www.justvape247.com/branded-concentrates-91-c.asp

http://www.astorwi.co.uk/?product=99

vapable.com

http://thee-cigshop.co.uk/DIY

http://decadentvapours.com/product.../connoisseur-range/

http://www.flavourart.co.uk/

http://www.totallywicked-eliquid.co.uk/.../flavour...

http://www.thealchemistscupboard.co.uk/product/capella

http://www.fsecig.com/mix.../eliquid-flavour-concentrates/

http://www.cloud9vaping.co.uk/FL10

http://www.vapedomain.co.uk/

http://www.vampirevape.co.uk/.../flavour-concentrates/

https://www.creamsupplies.co.uk/index.php?act=viewCat...

http://piratesvape.uk/

Lubrisolve:

T +44(0) 1458-259479
M +44(0) 7831-189311

e-mail: enquiries@lubrisolve.co.uk

http://www.liberty-flights.co.uk/products.asp

https://bigjuiceuk.co.uk

http://www.leisureliquids.com/?m=no

Equipment:

http://www.bottles4us.co.uk/

https://www.ibottles.co.uk/

http://www.wizardvapes.co.uk/

NOTES

NOTES

NOTES